Name: _____

MW00904327

Dinosaur Dot-to-Dot
Preschool Activity Book

by

Brynda Dunbar

Title: Dinosaur Dot-to-Dot Preschool Activity Book

ISBN 9798327161238

Copyright   2024 Brynda Dunbar

All rights reserved. No part of this publication may be reproduce, distributed, or transmitted in any form or by any means, including photocopying, recording, or other electronic or mechanical methods, without prior written permission of the publisher, except in the case of a brief quotations embodied in critical reviews and certain other noncommercial uses permitted by copyright law.

Thank You

I am Brynda Dunbar and I am a Coloring Book Artist and Creator. I create Coloring Books for all ages. My works have been used for Preschool children, Adults and even an people with dementia. Coloring has been known to induce Stress Relief and Relaxation.

Scan the QR Code below and it will take you to my Amazon Author Page where you can view all the current books that are available. I frequently add new content.

If you like what you see, please follow me, this will let you know when something new is added.

Thank you for taking the time to explore the wonderful world of coloring.

Brynda Dunbar

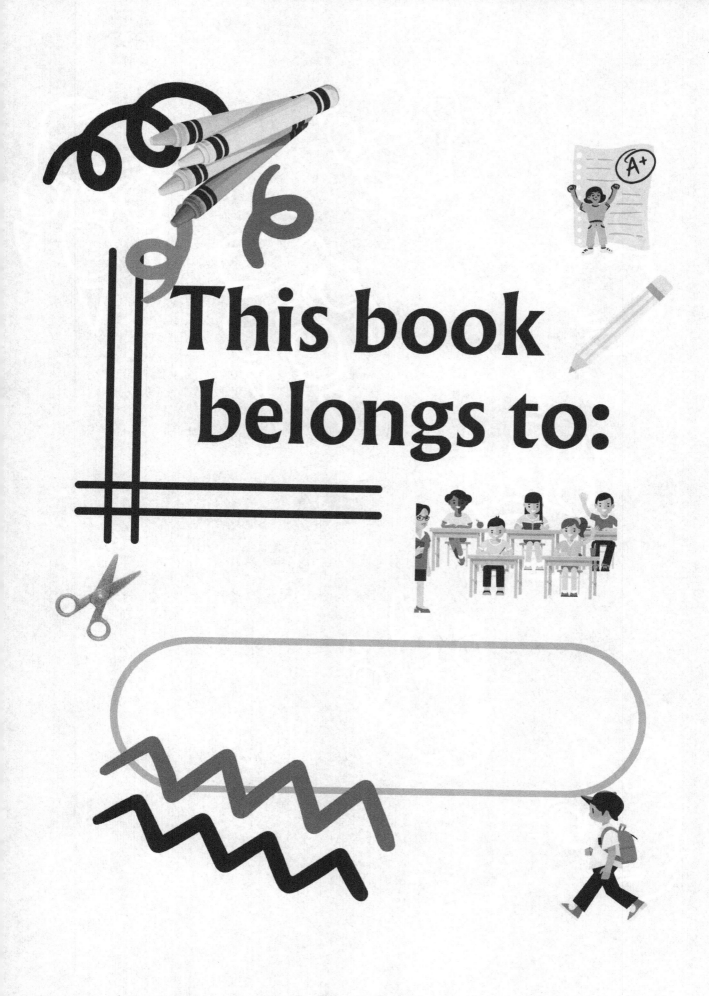

This book belongs to:

This page is for testing out media that you will be using in this book. I am placing a dark blank page after each design to assist with bleeding. If you want to make sure that there is no bleed thru, I would suggest that you place a piece of paper or cardstock behind the page to help prevent bleed thru.

COLOR TEST PAGES

Name:

Name:

Name:

Name:

Name: ∎━━━━━━━━━━∎

Name:

1

2

3

4

5

6

7

8

9

10

Name:

1

3

4

5

2

6

7

8

10   9

Name:

Name:

Name: ■━━━━━━━━━━━━■

Name:

Name:

Name:

Name: ■─────────────────■

Name: •━━━━━━━•

Name: ■━━━━━━━━━━━━━━━■

Name:

Name: ◼——————————◼

Name:

Name:

3 2 1

4

5

6

7

10 9 8

Name:

1
2
3
4
5   6   7
          8
              9
                10
                  11
                    12
                      13

Name:

Name: ■━━━━━━━━━━━■

Name: ∎━━━━━━━━∎

Name:

Name:

14   13   12 11 10   9   8   7   6   5   4   3   2   1

Name:

8

10

9 7

6

5

4

3

2

1

Name: ■━━━━━━■

Name:

1
2
3
4
5
6
7
10
8
9

Name:

10

7

9

8

6

5

4

3

2

1

Name:

Name:

8
9
7
10
6
5
3 4
2
1

Name:

Name: ∎━━━━━━∎

8

9

7

10

6

5

3 4

2

1

Name: ▪━━━━━━━━━▪

Name:

Name:

Dot Markers

Name: ▪━━━━━━━━━▪

Name:

Name: ▪——————▪

Name:

Name:

Name: ▪——————————▪

Name:

Name: _____

Name:

Name:

Congratulations
Good job

NAME:

You have completed this book with new skills!!!!!!

KEEP UP THE GOOD WORK

Thank You

Thank you for your purchase! If you have enjoyed this book, please consider dropping us a review. It takes 5 seconds and helps small businesses like ours.

The QR Code below will take you to your purchase.

Made in the USA
Las Vegas, NV
02 December 2024

13170997R00066